GYMNASTICS

Gymnastics Events

FLOOR, VAULT, BARS, AND BEAM

by Jen Jones

Consultant
Connie Dickson
Minnesota State Chair
USA Gymnastics Women's Program

Capstone
press

Mankato, Minnesota

Snap Books are published by Capstone Press,
151 Good Counsel Drive, P.O. Box 669, Mankato, Minnesota 56002.
www.capstonepress.com

Library of Congress Cataloging-in-Publication Data
Jones, Jen, 1976–
   Gymnastics events : floor, vault, bars, and beam / by Jen Jones.
   p. cm. — (Snap books. Gymnastics)
   Summary: "A guide for children and pre-teens on the events
at a gymnastics competition and the skills needed to excel in each
event"—Provided by publisher.
   Includes bibliographical references and index.
   ISBN-13: 978-0-7368-6469-5 (hardcover)
   ISBN-10: 0-7368-6469-5 (hardcover)
   1. Gymnastics—Juvenile literature. I. Title. II. Series.
GV461.3.J66 2007
796.44—dc22   2006002942

Editor: Wendy Dieker
Designers: Jennifer Bergstrom
Photo Researcher/Photo Editor: Kelly Garvin

Photo Credits: Capstone Press/Karon Dubke, cover; Corbis/Duomo, 23 (bottom left); Corbis/Neal Preston, 6–7, 12 (left); Corbis/Tom & Dee Ann McCarthy, 4–5; Corbis/Wally McNamee, 17 (right); Corbis Sygma/Ruszniewski J.Y., 23 (bottom right); Getty Images Inc./AFP/AF, 9 (right); Getty Images Inc./AFP/Mladen Antonov, 24–25; Getty Images Inc./AFP/Staff, 21 (right); Getty Images Inc./Bongarts/Christof Koepsel, 29; Getty Images Inc./Jamie Squire, 27; Jennifer Jones, 32; SportsChrome Inc./Michael Zito, 3, (all), 8–9 (left), 10–11, 12–13 (middle), 13 (right), 15, 17 (left), 19, 20–21 (left), 23 (top right, top left)

1 2 3 4 5 6 11 10 09 08 07 06

TABLE OF CONTENTS

Features

Event Excellence

Winning in competitive gymnastics is like trying to get straight As at school. In artistic gymnastics, women participate in four different gymnastics **events**. To be a top performer, gymnasts must do well in all of them. Among the events for females are floor exercise, vault, uneven bars, and balance beam. We'll learn more about each of them in this book.

Fab Floor
+ Vavoom Vault
+ Brilliant Bars
+ Beautiful Beam
= All-Around
Awesome!

During the events, many gymnastics skills are performed on each **apparatus**. Depending on a gymnast's strengths, she may be better at some events than others. For instance, an athlete with serious strength may excel on the uneven bars. But an athlete with personality and tumbling pizzazz might do best in the floor exercise. In this book, we'll see how to make the gymnastics "honor roll!"

5

1 Hit the Floor

Twists and tucks and layouts, oh my!

All kinds of advanced acrobatic skills can be seen in a typical floor exercise routine. Twists and layouts are just the beginning. In this event, gymnasts perform a series of tumbling runs. The "floor" is a large padded springy mat. Women's routines are set to music and feature dance movements. Gymnasts pick music that suits their personality. They try to woo the crowd and judges.

To be successful in floor exercise, a gymnast must master a variety of difficult tumbling skills. She must be able to land them all with ease. Most gymnasts do their hardest tumbling run first. That way they'll have maximum energy to nail it. Flexibility, confidence, and endurance also play a big role in how well a gymnast can pull off a floor routine.

Going for the Gold

In the floor exercise, gymnasts have just 70 to 90 seconds to show the judges their stuff. During that time, they must complete three or four tumbling runs. The harder the skills, the more points an athlete will rack up. However, with difficulty comes risk. Judges subtract points for skills done poorly. **Showmanship** is also important in scoring. Gymnasts try very hard to trade those grimaces for smiles!

"Everyone works hard, but only one person wins."
    –Yelena Davydova,
    Soviet Olympic medalist

1:15:03

Dominique Dawes

The 1996 U.S. Olympic women's gymnastic team packed a powerful punch. They nailed the All-Around team gold medal. One team member, Dominique Dawes, showed great promise in the floor exercise. Individually, Dominique Dawes' graceful floor routine landed her a bronze medal.

2 Vault into Victory

Great vaulters run like the wind and fly through the air!

Every vault stunt starts with a sprint down an 80-foot (25-meter) runway. The faster a gymnast can run, the more oomph her vault will have. After the running start, the gymnast jumps with both feet onto a springboard. She springs toward a padded table, using it to push off into the air. Those few seconds while the gymnast is in flight are used for flipping, twisting, and finally landing! Speed, strength, and height are the name of the game for a vault victory.

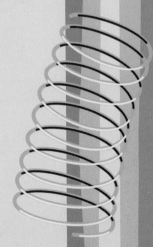

Vaulting History

* About 4,000 years ago, daredevils on the island of Crete once practiced "bull leaping." They attempted to grab a charging bull's horns, vault onto the bull's back, and safely dismount.

* In the early 1800s, vaulters used a wooden "horse," complete with head and tail.

* By the late 1800s, the horse's head and tail were gone, but the elongated body remained as the apparatus of choice.

* In 2001, the modern vault table was introduced in competition.

Going for the Gold

The types of vaults females can perform are divided into five categories. Judges watch for difficulty and how well the athlete approaches and **dismounts** the vault. The smoothness of the landing also counts in scoring. Deductions are taken if the gymnast takes a few steps or bends noticeably on the landing.

Mary Lou Retton

At the 1984 Olympic Games, Mary Lou Retton captured the first All-Around gold medal for a U.S. female gymnast. Crowds watched as she competed closely with Romanian gymnast Ecaterina Szabo. A perfect 10 on Retton's signature double full-twisting layout on the vault brought her sweet victory.

3 Don't Get Mad, Get Uneven

On the uneven bars, the saying "get a grip" takes on a whole new meaning!

The uneven bars consist of one thin bar about 7.5 feet (2.3 meters) from the ground. The second bar is about 5 feet (1.5 meters) up. In this event, gymnasts swing, turn, flip, and jump from one bar to the other without stopping. In order not to fall, a gymnast must rely on her sense of timing and distance. When the routine is complete, the gymnast dismounts with a flip or twist.

To get a better hold on the bars, athletes often "chalk up." Dipping their hands in a bowl of powdered chalk cuts down on sweat and reduces friction. Gymnasts also wear hand guards, or "grips," that help them hang on to the bar. Grips also protect gymnasts' hands from getting painful blisters.

GOING FOR THE GOLD

At 30 seconds long, routines on the uneven bars are shorter than some of the other events. To receive a high score, gymnasts must use both bars. They must perform skills such as turns and handstands, and change direction on the bar. All the while, they must appear graceful and calm. Piece of cake, right? If a gymnast falls or chooses an easy dismount, major points will be lost.

EARLY INNOVATOR

Doris Brause is one gymnast who knew how to go with the flow! In 1966, she was the first to perform a routine on the uneven bars without pausing, setting the standard for today's flowing routines.

Nadia Comaneci

In 1976, this young Romanian was the first athlete in Olympic history to score a perfect 10. Not too shabby for a 14-year-old! Her flawless performance on the uneven bars was enough to wow the judges. The uneven bar feat was just the beginning of her winning streak. Comaneci took home more than 21 gold medals throughout her career.

4 Beam Me Up

Ever try to walk on a tightrope? At only 4 inches (10 centimeters) wide, the balance beam doesn't have much more foot room. Amazing concentration and balance are needed to simply walk the length of the beam. Think of the skill needed to do handsprings, walkovers, ballet poses, and flips! It's not surprising that many consider the balance beam to be the sport's most challenging event.

To learn how to tumble on the beam, beginners often practice on the floor. A straight line of colored tape on the floor is the "beam." As a gymnast becomes more skilled with balance, she practices on a beam raised just slightly from the ground. She slowly works up to the real apparatus, which is 4 feet (1.2 meters) tall.

Going for the Gold

To stay atop the beam, gymnasts must display flawless control. Throughout the 70 to 90 second routine, a gymnast's feet must leave the beam at least twice for "flight elements" like leaps or flips. Equally important in scoring is the difficulty of the dismount. Taking the easy way off the beam costs points.

"Everyone gets scared, and everyone falls. The key is to get right back up and try again."
—Shannon Miller, U.S. Olympic medalist

Olga Korbut

Before the 1970s, Olympic gymnasts were usually about 20 years old and over 5 feet (1.5 meters) tall. But young Soviet gymnast Olga Korbut changed all that. At the 1972 Olympics in Munich, she was 17 years old. Her small frame and daring acrobatics left the crowd in awe. Olga performed the very first back somersault on the balance beam, helping her to earn three gold medals. She paved the way for tiny youngsters to compete at the top level.

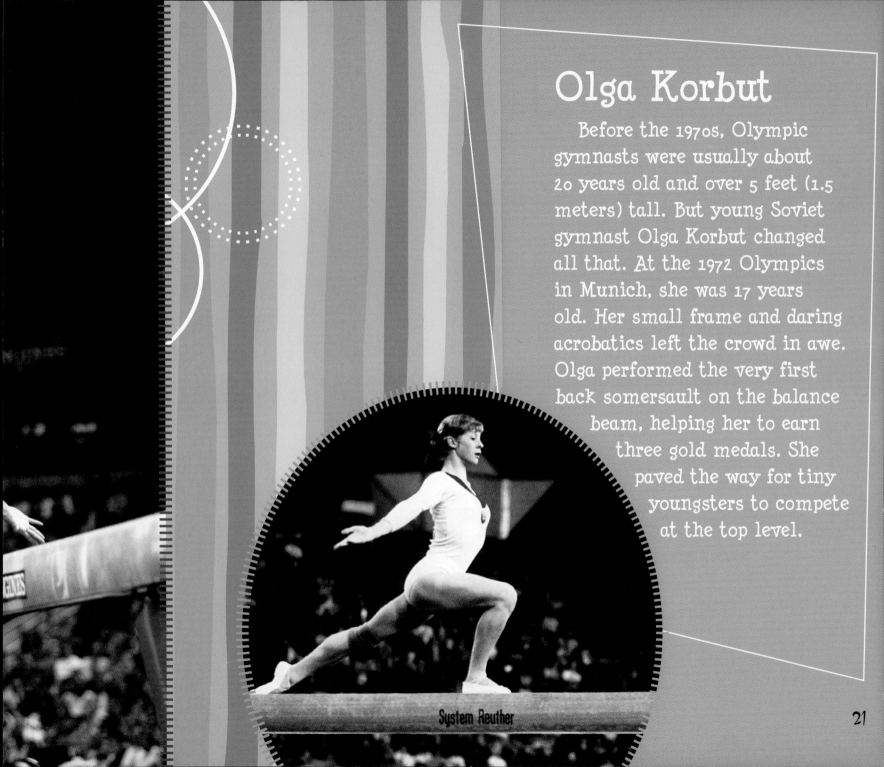

System Reuther

CHAPTER 5

Not Just a Girls' Sport

Men show their strong side in six artistic gymnastics events.

Female and male gymnasts perform many of the same tumbling skills in the floor exercise and vault. But men are the only ones who compete in the following four events.

In the **rings** event, men take hold of two rings that hang from the ceiling. They do handstands and hold poses between them.

In the **pommel horse** event, men mount a "horse" that has two handles, or "pommels." Supported by his hands, the gymnast swings, straddles, and scissors his legs over the length of the horse.

In the **horizontal bar** event, men do skills like somersaults and circles around a single raised bar. A difficult dismount finishes the routine.

On the **parallel bars**, men support themselves on two wooden rails that are next to each other. They hold poses that require a great deal of strength.

New Kids on the Block

Feel the Rhythm

Find out what's what in these three newer programs.

Let the music play! In the rhythmic gymnastics **program**, gymnasts put on their dancing shoes. Routines are set to music and feature the use of props. Hoops, balls, ropes, clubs, and ribbons help the gymnast make the show. As gymnasts throw, twirl, and leap through the props, beautiful patterns of colors are created.

In rhythmic gymnastics, athletes are judged on the difficulty and creativity with which the props are used. In fact, rhythmic gymnasts aren't even allowed to perform moves like flips and handsprings. Individual routines last 75 to 90 seconds. Group routines, with up to six people, are several minutes long. This event is very popular in Europe. However, it has yet to catch on with many competitive American gymnasts.

Lady and the Tramp

Since 1936, the trampoline has been making gymnasts jump for joy. However, trampolining has been an Olympic event only since 2000. Trampolines have long been viewed as a practice tool for budding gymnasts. But they are now a competitive apparatus used to perform breathtakingly high flips and skills.

In this program, gymnasts perform two routines. Each must include 10 skills such as baranis (half-twisting forward somersaults) and quadriffs (quadruple twisting somersaults).

Made in America

American gymnast and diver George Nissen built the first trampoline in his father's garage in 1936.

Two other variations of trampolining exist in competition. **Synchronized** trampoline features a pair of gymnasts. The duo perform identical movements at the same time. In the double-mini trampoline event, gymnasts take a running start. Similarly to the vault, they perform skills on two different trampolines before landing on a mat.

27

Amazing Acrobatics

Picture cheerleaders building a pyramid. Imagine circus acrobats creating a tower four people high. The balance skills performed in acrobatic gymnastics (or "acro") events often mirror these amazing feats. Using teamwork, gymnasts work in groups of two, three, or four to make pictures using their bodies. Talk about a balancing act! Gymnasts are judged on the stability and style of the exercises.

Something Old, Something New

The feats performed in acro date back to the ancient Egyptians. But this program has been a global gymnastics competition only since the 1970s.

With each new event and program, athletes are able to strut their stuff. Every gymnast can show off her skills in different ways. If you can show promise in many events, you might be ready to train for the gold in competitive gymnastics!

Glossary

apparatus (ap-uh-RAT-uhss)—equipment used in gymnastics, such as the balance beam or uneven bars

dismount (DISS-mount)—a move done to get off of an apparatus

event (i-VENT)—a category of competition; the four events in artistic gymnastics are balance beam, uneven bars, vault, and floor exercise.

program (PROH-gram)—a type of gymnastics; some programs include artistic, rhythmic, and acrobatic.

showmanship (SHOH-muhn-ship)—the ability to entertain a crowd

synchronized (SING-kruh-nized)—when two or more people perform the same movements at the same time

Fast Facts

On the Fast Track

Gymnasts were once literally on the fast track. In the first half of the 20th century, track and field events like rope climbing, pole vaulting, sprints, and shot put were considered gymnastics events.

Only Men

Even though women's gymnastics has become more popular, the women's events weren't featured at the Olympics until 1924.

Eat Your Wheaties

If you eat your Wheaties, you just might see a famous gymnast on the cereal box. Gold medalists that have graced the box in the past include Carly Patterson, Mary Lou Retton, and the 1996 Women's Olympic Team.

Read More

Ditchfield, Christin. *Gymnastics.* A True Book. New York: Children's Press, 2000.

Hughes, Morgan. *Gymnastics.* Junior Sports. Vero Beach, Fla.: Rourke, 2005.

Kalman, Bobbie. *Gymnastics in Action.* Sports in Action. New York: Crabtree, 2003.

Morley, Christine. *The Best Book of Gymnastics.* New York: Kingfisher, 2003.

Porter, David. *Winning Gymnastics for Girls.* New York: Facts on File, 2004.

Internet Sites

FactHound offers a safe, fun way to find Internet sites related to this book. All of the sites on FactHound have been researched by our staff.

Here's how:

1. Visit *www.facthound.com*

2. Choose your grade level.

3. Type in this book ID **0736864695** for age-appropriate sites. You may also browse subjects by clicking on letters, or by clicking on pictures and words.

4. Click on the **Fetch It** button.

Facthound will fetch the best sites for you!

About the Author

Jen Jones has been very involved in the cheerleading and gymnastics worlds since she was old enough to turn a cartwheel. Jen has several years of gymnastics training and spent seven years as a cheerleader. After college, Jen cheered and choreographed for the Chicago Lawmen semi-professional football dance team. Today Jen lives in Los Angeles and writes for publications like *Pilates Style*, *American Cheerleader*, and *Dance Spirit*. She also teaches cheerleading and dance classes and is a certified BalleCore instructor.

Index